TRIUMPH HOUSE
Poetry with a Purpose

INSPIRING FAITH

Edited by

CHRIS WALTON

First published in Great Britain in 1998 by
TRIUMPH HOUSE
1-2 Wainman Road, Woodston,
Peterborough, PE2 7BU
Telephone (01733) 230749

All Rights Reserved

Copyright Contributors 1998

HB ISBN 1 86161 211 7
SB ISBN 1 86161 216 8

Foreword

Over 90 Christian poets from all walks of life have joined hands to help spread the good word, whilst giving their views and experiences on things we hold close to our heart. Some of the poems tell a story, others express feelings and emotions, but all have a message to be shared and enjoyed by all.

Love, hope and faith in society today are just a few of the many subjects chosen, as the authors unite to form a single voice that reflects the views of Christians from all over the world.

With such a wide variety of views and opinions this anthology is a must for anybody in need of Christian inspiration.

Editor
Chris Walton

CONTENTS

1982	Susie Barker	1
Frustration	Jacqui Short	2
Father - Son	Lynne Barker	3
Men Of Faith	Michael R Bending	4
No One	K Scarfe	5
Dark Glass	Hilary Trenholme	6
Prayer For Assurance	Karen Lawrence	7
In The Image Of God	John Pepper	8
Too Late	Jan Caswell	9
Joyride	Peter Burton	10
Gorilla, Gorilla On The Wall	B Rankin	11
Doubt (A Pledge)	Mark R Keen	12
Wasted Life	Rae Fulton	13
After An Unwilling Visit To An Army Museum	Charmian Goldwyn	14
Blame Who!	Graham Griffiths	16
Let Us Beware	Nancy Cooper	18
Wealth	Veronica Rowlands	19
What If	Josephine Gander	20
Retirement	E Walker	22
The Final Question	J S Maidwell	23
Message Of The Bells	Sidney Talbot	24
And From My Tongue Shall Come His Words And Works	Anthony le Feuvre	25
Half A Life	Kirsty Clarke	26
Life	Kwan Phung	27
Digging For Faith	R J Priest	28
Angel	R Carpenter	29
The Fad Eternal	Phoenix Martin	30
Reflections Of Society	Martyn Harrison	31
Apathy	Sandy Thomson	32
The Stone	John Wiltshire	33
Just Look Around	Dora Beswick	34
People At Prayer	Brenda K Bunce	35
Society	Dan Chellumben	36
Ivy Holme	Robert V Anthony	37

For Peace	Mary Mudge	38
What About The Children	Naomi Frost	39
Questions	Maud Boreham	40
I'll Share Your Burden	Ann Willbourne	41
Thank God For God	Lyn Coker	42
Two Halves Of The Same	Kieran Coor	43
The Flotsam And Jetsam Of Life	Vicki Robinson	44
Thoughts At A Concert	Stella Shepherd	45
The Roundabout Or Where Are We Going	Barbara Collier	46
Peace In Our Time	Maureen Quirey	47
Face To Face	Ruth Daviat	48
Faith	John Farrell	49
The Most Beautiful Word	Warren Galley	50
Poverty	Bridget Holding	51
Break Bread Together	Eleanor Clarke	52
Along The Way . . .	Andrea Noelle Vaughan	53
Two Sides For Living	Joy Spickermann	54
I Am	Porter Duff	55
Trust In My Society	Margaret Gleeson Spanos	56
Anthony	Trebor Lien	57
Never Mine	Maureen Mills	58
The Grey Generation	Joyce Goldie	59
Life's Goal	Malcolm F Rowlatt	60
Man Destroys Man	Christine Miller	61
Just Look Around	Jacqueline Sanderson	62
The World	James McErlean	63
Hear My Prayer	Audrey Walker	64
Insight	D F Baker	65
A Changed Society	Shirley Hay	66
Sweet Vine Of Life	Cassandra Hazeley-Wilson	68
Tomorrow's World	Christina Crowe	69
A Song For Lonely Hearts	Gail Farrell	70
My Christian Faith	Michael John Swain	71
The Preacher	Ann G Wallace	72
Reflections	Pauline Wilkins	74
I Wonder	Susan Goldsmith	75

Unrobed In Ulster	Peter Taylor	76
Contemporary Commination	Trudi Yates Morgan	77
Changing For The Better	Twinny	78
God's Plan Was Perfect	Vera G Taylor	79
Our Modern Age	Dorothy Headland	80
Watermark	Tom Griffiths	81
A Dream For Us All	Jane Smith	82
What Is Important	Wendy Brennan	83
World Vision	Rosetta Stone	84
Marriage	Jean Hendrie	86
God Only Knows	Anthony Stern	87
Will The World?	Samantha Douglas	88
Circle Of Light	B J Tallowin	89
Forgiveness	Jennifer Brewer	90
Twelve Days Of Xmas	David Atkinson	91
Reality	Pam Lewis	92
Think Of Tomorrow	Evelyn Ingram	93
A Fear Of The Future	Deborah Carol Hughes	94
Friend	Trevor Brammah	95
Peace - Perfect Peace	Monica O'Sullivan	96
Innocent Eyes	Marjorie Boyes	97
Don't Ever Look Back	J Robinson	98
House Builders	Stephen Eric Smyth	99
Our Society	Linda A Brown	100

1982

And where was God today? Not here with us,
The devastating noise and then -
The silence it evoked - before the rush of
Agonising screams, the dreadful sounds,
Of people sighing, moaning, crying, bleeding,
Dying, their bodies wracked in pain, mutilated,
Limbs torn from them, - Christ -
These bloodied jumbled heaps of lifeless rag,
A large and unsolved human jigsaw, crushed,
Fragmented in this cruel and graceless grave,
Happy in their separate ways, a minute past,
And where was God today? Not here with us!

And where was God today? Not here with us,
With aching heart and trembling hand I knelt
To help, in what small way, I, useless could!
A choking layer of dust had filled our lungs,
The smoke and flames grew nearer, yet more close,
And all the doctors, nurses and police,
Were working fast,
A woman close at hand, said - 'do not fret -
It is God's way' - I choked within,
Clenched my fist, bit on dust - but
Could not say - and
Where was God today - not here with us.

Susie Barker

FRUSTRATION

Excuse me - it is me who is talking,
I am sitting down here in this chair,
You talk about me to the person who is pushing
Just as if I wasn't here.

Have you any idea how frustrating that is
And the humiliation I feel?
Just because my body is somewhat disabled
Doesn't mean I am mentally ill.

Also, we need to go shopping,
But there's so many shops out of bounds,
If our wheelchairs get caught up with boxes and such
Then we have to put up with the frowns.

Shops can lose lots of custom
By keeping us out of their stores,
All we want is to shop like everyone else
So, please, can they just clear the floors.

We cannot get through very narrow doors,
We need them a little bit wide,
For, apart from the seat we are sitting in
There are wheels jutting out at each side.

For us, many things are limited,
Where we go - and what we can do,
So, please won't you lend us a helping hand,
There are plenty of things you can do.

If you were to spend a whole day in a wheelchair,
Many pitfalls you'd find you'd go through,
Only then can you realise the help that is needed
To help us live just as you do.

Jacqui Short

FATHER - SON

What's so special? What can God do?
I've got one father, I don't need two.
I can't see Him, He doesn't play ball
I wonder whether He's there at all.
And if He's there - how does He know me?
I haven't sent a letter or been on TV.

He's always there, He's always been
He's always kind, and never mean.
He'll come and help if you ask Him to.
He'll be with you your whole life through.
I'm here to help with earthly things -
To catch your ball, to push your swings.

I'm here to give advice or hugs,
To nurse you through those nasty bugs.
I try my best, but try as I might
We both know I'm not always right.
He's number one without even trying -
He gave His Son to save us from dying.

Lynne Barker

MEN OF FAITH

He let his teardrops soak into the page,
His wish, was that they'd print it as a whole.
This piece was written down in fitful rage,
If he'd believed in God, he'd bared his soul
To anyone who really read his word.

His family was precious, yet he'd dared
To speak his mind. The danger now increased,
All sides might try to harm them, though he cared,
He could not quit until the killings ceased.
Damn the risk! He knew he must be heard.

One man of faith, had faced the world to say,
That he'd not rest, until *his* faith had won.
The object of his hatred said, that day.
'My faith insists, that your peace *I* must shun,
Even talking to you seems absurd!'

Mystified by gestures such as these,
Such firm belief from each, to him seemed odd,
The non-believer, sank down to his knees,
To ask *'How can they worship the same God*
Whilst living lives by hatred stirred?'

Michael R Bending

NO ONE

I pleaded my case, I tried to explain,
But no one cared and no one came.
I had a reason, couldn't you see?
Why would no one listen to me?

I did my best to put it right,
Screaming uselessly into the night.
So what was the point when no one heard?
And no one's conscience even stirred?

Just heartless inhumanity,
No one dared to look and see
At all the problems all around,
But on sympathy's ear made no sound.

So here I wait for the axe to fall,
No one to ring, no one to call.
If anyone cared then they would know,
But no one came by for me to show.

It's so unjust, so unfair
And oh so cold when no one's there.
I could have guessed, I should have seen
What happens when man is replaced by machine!

K Scarfe

DARK GLASS

Yes, there is crime. Yes there is fear.
And, in our time, TV makes it clear.
Yes, there is pain and it's very widespread.
But once there was Cain and a brother was dead.

Once there were stocks and ducking stools,
Boiling oil shocks and torturing tools.
There were boys in chimneys and toiling in mines,
There were ploys for extortion, flogging and fines.

There was no saving, no help from the state -
There was no raving, just acceptance of fate.
Life was raw with no hope to the end,
With every door shut between victim and friend.

Yes there is crime, but there is so much support
Of life's climb uphill, as battles are fought.
There is the hand of concern from the many who care,
Whilst life's big demand has more fairness to share.

Hilary Trenholme

PRAYER FOR ASSURANCE

Dear Jesus when You showed me
The path I had to tread,
My soul it leapt within me,
But my body filled with dread.
The life I've led
Has left me hard,
Anxiety has ruled.
The only true and honest way
Is dependence on the Lord.
But fear in living,
The thought of giving
All I have - though little -
Is sometimes hardest of all,
When most I've had is pity.

Now through Your Word, the Bible,
Lord Jesus speak to me,
And give me the assurance
I need so desperately.

Karen Lawrence

IN THE IMAGE OF GOD

Being creative involves cultivating soil, curiosity, and friendships;
Being creative involves the birth of a child, and a poem;
Being creative involves the development of physical prowess, photographic material, and understanding;
Being creative involves uniting with the natural world to produce food, clothes, housing, transport, and medicine.

To create is to suffer.

Creation may allow us a glimpse of the holiness of beauty,
and the beauty of holiness.

Creation means being true to ourselves and to the One who made us.

Being creative means Being.

John Pepper

Too Late

    Golden sands untouched by human hands
    Shimmer beneath unconquered cliffs.
    Below fast rolling tides seethe with silver fish.
    Above on outstretched wings white sea birds soar
    Filling the summer air with high-pitched cries.
Acrid wastes seep ever onwards to the sea, but
Ignorance no longer an excuse for man.
Drop by drop the creeping menace flows unfettered.
Sunbaked beaches sullied before his eyes.

    White fleecy clouds in azure skies
    Float softly by on gentle breeze
    And laughter blends with bird song sweet.
    The soul of man stirs in fervent expectation
    As clear air permeates the hidden depths.
Decadent man fails to seek the truth, so
Rabid in his desire to gain the upperhand.
Unrepentant he continues his daily spoilage.
Gaseous exhaust fumes rise ever upwards.
Spectacular sunsets betraying his misdemeanours.

    God's good earth yields many treasures
    Through earthquake, wind and fire.
    His harvest's full of plenty for nations side by side.
    The human heart should swell with pride to be God's chosen one.
    To share these gifts with everyone and join His saints in heaven.
Abominations manifest themselves.
Barriers no longer stop the rampant infestations and
Uncontrolled, victims soon succumb.
Sanctions come too late to rectify the mess, so
Enlightened man must wallow in the mire of his own greed.

Jan Caswell

JOYRIDE

Twisted body crumpled and torn
An angel no longer alive
Taken from life by three creatures from hell
She was four, she would never be five.

Not for her the sweet joys of childhood
Nor the gift of a child of her own
Just a dark, lonely grave now awaits her
And an epitaph chiselled on stone.

'It was just for a laugh,' said the guilty
'Just a joyride, we needed a thrill
We never intended to hurt her
We never intended to kill.'

So a smack on the wrists for the culprits
Maybe send them away for a year.
They'll make better men, never do it again
And society's conscience is clear.

Now a young mother's arms are empty
But her heart's overflowing with pain
You can lose many things in a lifetime
But some memories will always remain.

Peter Burton

GORILLA, GORILLA ON THE WALL

He stubbed out his cigar in the ashtray
As he turned away he thought he heard a scream
He put on his raincoat and melted into the city
His image squeaky clean.
It was early evening in Africa and a poacher with hungry eyes.
Threw his shadow at a silhouette and a gentle giant died.

All animals show token resistance more instinct than understanding
Gone are the days of roaming free, eating, sleeping and grazing
Because with man's whim to boost up his ego
And the need for more land to grow food.
The imbalance is becoming alarming
And the slaughtering machine more crude.

Far away from Africa, in the cities of bright lights
Oblivious to what is happening in Africa, and the endless sacrifices
Man's greed and lack of concern, pour from the television screen
The night closes in in Africa again
The air is full of sickening screams.

The cigar smoulders in the ashtray
That once deftly climbed trees
Attached to a gentle giant's body
Soon severed by man's disease
Our man has a potion made of rhino horn
That breeds insatiable lust
And a once proud gorilla's head looks down from the wall in disgust.

You can still see the pain in his eyes
Alas now frozen forever
We still have time to end this nightmare
It's better late than never.

B Rankin

DOUBT (A PLEDGE)

Doubt is a tumour of the heart
One for which no cure can be found
Save that which one experienced in the art
Of such matters
Can employ
Namely love

It is my devout intention
Barring acts of God and the like
To administer this remedy to you
In the prescribed dosage
And at the prescribed times
Until such time
As the tumour does abate
And you are once again
No longer afflicted by this malady.

Mark R Keen

WASTED LIFE

At this moment in time your life's in a mess, why have
you lost so much happiness.
You say that you love but where's the respect, the two
go together you haven't leant yet.
The answer doesn't lie at the bottom of a glass, or the
quick fix you take to blow out your mind.
What are you really expecting to find
And dealing it out well, that's even worse, young
lives destroyed, Oh what a curse.
Take a look at yourself, what do you see, you're not
the same person who once looked at me.
You've thrown it away and don't seem to care, all
that's left is an empty stare.
Don't tread the path that you trod before, are you
really so stupid to go back for more.
Sort yourself out before it's too late, don't fill
your life with sorrow and waste.
Kindness and love is all that we gave, so why
have you started digging your grave.
Nothing is ever really that bad, life is too
short to be empty and sad.
But if that's what you want and you're not
going to try, the best we can do is just say 'Goodbye.'

Rae Fulton

AFTER AN UNWILLING VISIT TO AN ARMY MUSEUM

Why must one people oppress another?
People A feel superior to people B
Have more guns
Make Bs speak their language
Follow their rules.
Change their religion.

Tax them.
Build prisons to put them in
If they don't pay taxes
Or follow their laws.

People B feel frustrated
Want their own language
Own Rules
Own Religion
Own land.
A leader leaps up
'I will lead you to *Freedom!*'

War.
Many people killed.
Men, women, children
Old folk, babies.
Fear
Illness
Starvation.

Now if people B win . . .
What next
Depends on the leader who needs to be
Above Reproach
Above Cupidity
Above Corruption.

You don't see many of those about.

Where did it start?
When will it end?

Weapons themselves have become
Objects of worship.
Aren't we clever?
Small boys play with toy tanks and guns
Never thinking
That one day
Their family may be killed
By the monstrous distorted icons of war.

Charmian Goldwyn

BLAME WHO!

A bush fire burns, two boys run away.
Destroying the habitat, their idea of play.
No thought of wrong-doing, just having a laugh.
Parental guidance, education. A farce!

Where is your child at this moment? Who cares?
I'm playing bingo, I'm counting my shares.
I'm off to a dinner-dance, I'm off down the pub.
I'm watching television, I'm golfing at the club.

To hell with the environment, my life must come first.
My children wouldn't do that. No fun in scorched earth.
What harm has been done? Some bushes, a few trees,
They'll grow back in time, covered in leaves.

Prosecute! What for? More harm done with wars.
Take Sellafield, oil tankers, open-casts and roads.
Yes it was stupid; I would never condone.
But then how many sinners would cast the first stone?

With a society that's corrupt and an establishment near worse,
Our children stand no chance to learn what is worth.
No discipline, no guidance, no respect either way.
Sodom and Gomorra are here, and will stay.

Until administrators return to honesty and goodwill,
With respect for the electorate who picks up the 'bill'.
And the church, a ship, that has now gone aground,
Should clear its decks of all deviance that abounds.

Is it any wonder that our children run wild,
When all they can see is corruption on all sides.
Government, big business, much judiciary too,
With hands in the 'till' while turning the screw.

Milking the British cow until it drops dead,
Then on to the farm of third worlds, more profit, new beds.
Lies, innuendo. 'We are innocent!' They cry.
From the deepest of sewers their excuses now fly.

No honour, no conscience, no thoughts of treason,
Profit from arms' sales is a good enough reason
To deal with the enemy, to allow greed to drive on.
Modern day politics leading to Armageddon.

Graham Griffiths

LET US BEWARE

In the year 2040, I certainly won't be here
But will the birds be singing 'cause they're beginning to disappear
Are we all too busy racing from here to there
To notice how, instead of green, concrete is everywhere
With our car we travel miles and miles to see a pretty place
Then in move the developers and it's gone without a trace
Never mind the wildlife, the insects and the birds
But how could we destroy them? It's just too sad for words.

We have many, many highways with traffic very dense
Often grinding to a halt, does it really make any sense?
Travelling down a country lane the views will bring delight
Until I see the dead things that are killed by speed at night
A mangled blackbird lying there was looking for some food
We haven't just killed her, we have also killed her brood
There's another menace that we have to keep in view
And that's our little feline friends, but yes, I love them too
However, with their winning ways we have fallen for their charm
And although they diminish rats and mice, the birds do come to harm.

Now lets look at farming, no hedges and sprayed fields
Feeding cows with offal anything goes to improve the yields
We once thought we would increase the crops by spraying DDT
It stayed in the ground for many years, did it come back to you and me?
We have heard of all the illnesses, asthma, salmonella, BSE
How all this has come about is very clear to see
We can't destroy the very things we eat and drink
Because our food is important and illness has a link
Nobody owns anything we are caretakers of this land
And many of us do our best giving nature a helping hand.

Thank goodness for the experts who safeguard our legacy
But we must be aware, many things depend on you and me.

Nancy Cooper

WEALTH

This world of opposites hems me in
And makes me think I'm rich, or poor,
But what is considered to be my wealth?
Is it money, possessions and that which I own?
Material wealth whatever it's kind
Is judged by that personal thinking mind.
Only thought can bring this about,
So you gather, collect and show it off
Because if it's wanted by others like you,
Then the object you own has relative value.

But if for a moment you impersonalise,
You will suddenly experience what it is to be wise.
There is no such thing as 'yours' and 'mine',
For all that exists is One and Divine.
You are put in charge of certain things
To look after and cherish for a short space in time.
You cannot possess that which is not yours,
You cannot clutch air in the palm of your hand,
Or a handful of sun or water, or wind.
Be released from the opposites which never began.

No poverty ever can any one have
When you are that One fulfilling all Love.
So 'I', like you who is also name 'I',
Possess all the riches of earth and the sky.

Veronica Rowlands

WHAT IF

Once more the slumbering earth stirs,
Again hues of green and gold are to be hers,
To Prince Hope anew she will give birth,
Smiling we will welcome a new infant to the earth.

What if the bells of spring should no longer ring,
What if heralding birds should no longer sing,
What if Mother Earth should shed a tear,
For sleeping bulbs in their earthly tomb,
What if woman should grieve for babes stilled in the womb.

What if fragrant rose should no longer bloom
What if the smell of fear pervade this earthly ruin,
What if the lonely bee no summer flower should find,
Then how would the weeping creator view mankind.

What if there should be no ripening corn,
What if there should be no joyful morn,
What if there should be deadly acid rain,
A gift to us from the powerful insane.

What if there should be no six-pointed stars of white,
Silently falling in the night,
Only a skeleton child, pale with fright,
Huddled in fear, no possibility of flight.

What if golden-haired with child,
Should rend the air with screams wild,
Love gave me this treasure so rare,
Was I wrong to accept such a gift without a care.

Beware mad *man*, whose power-hungry eyes,
Now seeks a charred, dying planet as prize,
Look you who will not the dreadful picture see,
Quickly come listen to our womanly please,
Arise join us before it is too late,
Let us cast out this legacy of hate.

Josephine Gander

Retirement

Don't dwell on the reverse side of things
The sleepless nights and rheumy twinges,
The days when headaches seem the 'norm'.
The winter battle to keep one warm.
Worst of all, time takes toll of friends
As their time on earth comes to an end.

Today was a good day, as days go -
The good things come thick and fast you know.
It's all or nothing, don't you agree?
In the quirky way of things, it seems to me.
No rushing about because we're late.
No traffic jam in which to wait.
A 'free' parking spot close to town.
A choice of sandwich (and a can to wash it down)
Eaten in the park beside the flowers,
A pleasant way to spend the hours.

So take a stick and a scarf, don country shoes
Walk up the hill to admire the views.
These are the 'plusses' of retirement.
Take each day as it comes and *be content.*

E Walker

THE FINAL QUESTION

When the trees are leafless,
When flowing streams run dry,
When the seas are poisoned,
When pollution fills the sky.

When the hills stand barren,
When death stalks through the land,
When man's shattered cities
Lie buried in the sand.

When the whales and dolphins
Are all on butcher's hooks.
When rhinos, tigers, leopards,
Are only seen in books.

When the flowers have withered,
When birds have ceased their song:
We'll seek surviving scientists
And ask them: 'What went wrong?'

J S Maidwell

MESSAGE OF THE BELLS

Think of our church and its fine set of bells
And the glorious message that each peal foretells
They will joyfully celebrate the day we are wed
Just as the solitary toll declares the day we are dead.
If we had been invaded the bells would have rang
But victory was ours, in the end we all sang!

Over meadows and fields we have heard many peels
From distant churches this lovely sound steals.
Every sound is so different but each message the same
Whether from a great city or a quiet country lane.
In days gone by ringing was all part of living
It was music to all, it was their thanksgiving.

At the end of the year the bells welcome the new
As we await the first service in our church pew.
At Christmas the bells joyfully tell of the birth
And at harvest say thanks for the bounteous earth.
The bell ringers below know what ringing's about
So we say 'Thank you all, for the message sent out.'

Sidney Talbot

AND FROM MY TONGUE SHALL COME HIS WORDS AND WORKS

Who can speak for the illness in this world?
Come forward the mind of God. Come forward.
The hurricane breaks your house, can't you see?
Then leap, yourself, over your sleeping lords
and counsel your nature before she leaves.
The tundra and desert take our cities,
the planets keep quiet, no wonders arrive,
Then visit, yourself, descend to the earth
and punish the monsoon skipping with spite
and shock senseless laughter into care.
What animal form has the human become?
shall we turn away from the flooding death?
Shall we ignore? No, the soul is of God
and from my tongue shall come His words and work.

Anthony le Feuvre

HALF A LIFE

Awash with emotion
I feel your spirit near.
Reaching out,
just to show you care.

Your love knows no boundaries,
good and true are your words.
For those that wish to listen,
joyous sounds shall be heard.

Half a life is who we are,
incomplete is how we feel.
To be whole we must take up the faith,
or else half a life is the deal what we make.

Kirsty Clarke

LIFE

Indestructible as stone
unable to get out of shape
never weeps or moans
anything life throws at it, it can take.
Edges as sharp as a head of a pin
sides like a cold and hard shell
but is it like that within?
From outside no one can tell.
Relied on to hold things erect
not appreciated as it stands through wind and rain
as it's taken for granted not to have any sort of defect
but could it withstand a hurricane?
As many years go by
its coat gets slowly slowly worn
it's a cruel and painful way to die
now eroded to dust it wonders why it was born.
It has done what past stones have done
only to realise it has been used
finding out its time on earth could have been fun
but instead it allowed itself to be abused
expecting its accomplishments to be looked up to
expecting fellow stones to turn green
but that's not what they do
as the same kind of work stretches as far as can be seen.
Now stripped of its outer coat
exposed for all the world to see
its spirit hums a wistful note
as it regrets how it paid its fee.

Kwan Phung

DIGGING FOR FAITH

From Jericho to Jerusalem, man searches high and low.
He turns the stone, digging deep, sifting with a hoe.
Finding the clues, waiting for the world to know,
'This is not enough,' he says 'I need more proof to show.'
The holy spirit seeks the man but he remains aloof,
Man searches over biblical text for arguments of truth.
Then he asks the elders for they are so wise.
A simple statement spoken, remove scales from thine eyes
His eyes seek low, His eyes seek high, but always just behind,
The holy spirit waits by him, all in God's own time
He shouts up to the Lord, 'Where then is my proof?'
The Lord says 'Seek with heart, not eyes, there will be the truth.'
The man rails and shouts aloud, 'Is this then a ruse?'
'My name is God, not Satan. My son was slain for you.'
'Where, then, is your son upon the earth, I cannot see him anywhere?'
'He's left the world in physical form. He now moves through the air.'
'I cannot see this lord, so I take it upon faith
I give myself to Jesus, saviour of our race.'
The Lord smiles down upon him and through his only son
Fills man with the spirit. It's work has just begun.

R J Priest

ANGEL

Lord, send me an angel,
To help us fix this mess.
The workload's too much for a priest.
We need more than forgiveness.

So Lord, send me an angel,
This cross is too much to bear.
I need to lay my burden down,
Have you got one to spare?

I wouldn't need him very long,
So, dear Lord, hear my plea.
I need a helping hand,
Please send an angel down to me.

I know that you are busy,
Righting all the wrongs we do.
Sometimes I despair,
I guess we must disappoint you.

But if you sent an angel,
Maybe he could help us see.
Then we wouldn't need to bother you.
We'd all live in harmony.

So Lord, send me an angel,
To lead us through this maze.
After all, they're always telling us,
You work in mysterious ways!

But, then again, just maybe,
He's already here, right now.
For each person who learns to love,
Perhaps he's teaching how.

R Carpenter

THE FAD ETERNAL

Our souls recoil from their dead attacking eyes
which seem to pierce the everyday defences.
They're not interested in niceties, nor kindness, nor lies -
they act, destroy and damn the consequences.

Their world's a Dantean chaos, full of pain -
a cosmos of deprivation - aggression
being the one point of control, their sole ration of power
in an existence of stagnant impotence.

They frighten us - we don't want to see their wounds.
Content, complacent, we wend our lazy way
to life's end, comfortable in our own box with our allotted doom -
frail, pretty flies waiting for the end of May.

Still they lounge against the wall, hide not their scorn
of all that is organised, all that is us
and we, in our wisdom, condemn them for a violence born
of rebellion against established bias.

Yet this traditional prejudice prevails -
the suit and tie doctrine of a tired old age
and no matter how often new generation's revolt fails
somehow youth always assaults this gilded cage
and vandals are just another facet of the fad eternal.

Phoenix Martin

REFLECTIONS OF SOCIETY

Can't look in the mirror,
It scares me,
Seeing reflections of society.
Scenes of fighting,
Scenes of lies.
While someone laughs,
Another cries.

Martyn Harrison

APATHY

If Hitler was alive today
and building up his bold array,
would all of us stand still and meek
And watch him overrun the weak?

If Jesus was alive today
would we be more inclined to pray?
Or would we consciously look blank
and label him another crank?

If JFK was here today
to steer the mighty USA,
would missiles lurk behind each hill
and Vietnam be burning still?

If Nelson was alive today
en route towards Trafalgar's fray,
would he plan reconciliations
or carronades for warring nations?

If Stalin was alive today
to see his system in decay,
would he ignore the people's pain
and fill the labour camps again?

If Chairman Mao was here today
would all his children gaily play?
Or would they face grenades and flares
defying tanks in city squares?

If all mankind were dead today
then Mother Earth would have to say
farewell to all humanity.
Not through neglect but apathy.

Sandy Thomson

THE STONE

Life is a stone
thrown by a child
that strikes the sea.
A splash - a few ripples
and then the sea
is once more
the same,
as if the stone had never left
the hand that threw it.
The sea - and I
What will we leave
that will be remembered
when the sea no longer
winces and is still?
Will it be music,
that dies at birth
yet lives for ever?
A painting born at the death
of some great nobody?
Or perhaps the memory
of some great battle
that killed the world?
The world that couldn't
even remember why it fought.

John Wiltshire

JUST LOOK AROUND

How can we be sure of life?
Just look around.
The mare with her foal, enjoying every minute,
As they frolic together.
Eating the grass, all the goodness it,
Comes from the ground.

How can we be so sure of life?
Just look around
Sheep with their lambs, cows with their calves
They each know their own
Mother Nature takes care of the needs of the dams
It comes from the ground.

How can we be so sure of life?
Just look around,
Cars with their petrol, ships with their oil,
Aeroplanes flying high
Industry grows faster, when workers will toil
For wealth from the ground.

How can we be so sure of life?
Just look around.
The children at play with their mums and their dads,
The happiest time of all
As they grow into healthy lasses and lads.
With food from the ground.

Yes, we can be sure of life
If we take care of the ground.

Dora Beswick

PEOPLE AT PRAYER

People at prayer is not new,
Nowadays they are all too few,
Baptist, Methodist,
Congregationalist,
There are many more on the list.

Without the others the bigger ones,
Whose congregations out number some,
Roman Catholic,
Church in Wales,
Church of England, Songs of Praise.

Pearls of wisdom are there somewhere,
But most of the people just don't care,
Too busy drinking,
And watching TV,
To care about Jesus and God's country.

That is why the churches are small,
People are not trying, not trying at all,
To make them bigger,
To make them hold on,
You've to do the right thing now, not the wrong.

Brenda K Bunce

SOCIETY

Society is rapidly going downhill
We are increasingly disregarding God's will
With no thought given to his teachings.

Since our needs, religion is not filling,
In technology we now seek solace
For the standards of living it raises
To prolong life it conquers disease
And despite many other positive effects it creates
Man's capacity for evil it increases
Social ills consequently hit a new high
We are more violent, more callous and more careless
Domestic violence, broken marriage, abandoned children,
                                          child prostitution
Plays havoc with our civilisation
People depend upon drugs to relieve their ailments
Even children are given tranquillisers in the classroom
Because of a fictitious condition called hyperactivity

More and more working couples find no time for a true family life
That teenagers are troubled for missing their parents a lot
Thousands of the city's youth belong to gangs
Pollution, poverty, organised crime, unemployment, homelessness
Politicians, scientists, economists have not seriously handled
Even the millions of pounds and countless hours spent
Have proved to no avail
These problems now plaguing us
Are a big challenge for the coming generations.

It is high time we rebuilt a society without insanity
Without war and without criminality
Where anybody can prosper
And honest beings can have rights
Where man is free to rise to greater heights
As we approach the year 2000.

Dan Chellumben

IVY HOLME

Swings stood drenched in a playground
Children no longer there
Hurried home for shelter
And a mother's waiting care
But then one sees a movement
A swing still on the go
A boy alone is swinging
He's no desire to leave
His eyes are dark and listless
The sparkle gone so soon
His movements are pathetic
His home is out of tune
No longer sounds of laughter
To fill its spacious rooms.

Robert V Anthony

FOR PEACE

Damaged lives all around
Spirits broken know no bounds
Death brings its final sleep
For these people we should weep.

Stopped in life's full flow
Hatred of man towards his foe
Others on sidelines stand
Offer no helping hand.

But human spirit should rise above this
And be prepared to take the risk
To help the forms that lie upon the floor
We should not stand by and allow it to be more.

World-wide our stand we should make
Against the evil like rattlesnake
Stand up for what is right not wrong
And make it mankind's worldly song.

Let justice be seen and seen to be done
In daily tasks leave none undone
May honour be our byword and care be our aim
And as the human race united, our heads held high again.

Mary Mudge

WHAT ABOUT THE CHILDREN

What about the children?
Who'll spare a thought for them?
Must they suffer on in silence
In these brutal wars of men?
These men whose quests for glory,
Spurred on by greed and power,
Kill and maim the children,
In their deepest, blackest hour.
Trample down the walls of innocence.
Destroy the gift of life.
Terrorise; dehumanise.
Ferocity so rife.
What about the children?
Spare a thought for them.
As their precious years of childhood
Die - in these brutal wars of men.

Naomi Frost

QUESTIONS

See this book, Gran, from upstairs
It's got things called polar bears.
Did they *really* run free
In other lands across the sea?
What are these, Gran, what are seals?
Their eyes look big as catherine wheels.
Look at these, it calls them whales
Great big fish with funny tales.

All these things that swam and flew
Did they live in our world too?
If they'd been on earth so long,
What *did* happen - what went wrong?
Those elephants up on your shelf,
Did you see *real* ones for yourself?
You told me owls lived in the barn
I haven't seen them on the farm.

You said they flew without a sound
Why aren't there any more around?
What happened then - who made them go?
Tell me, Gran, 'cause *you* must know
If 'Pollution' was the man
Then tell me why he did it, Gran.
You tell me stories - show me books
It's not the same as *proper* looks.

Why d'you say we'll never learn?
I've been to school for half a term.
Teacher says I'm 'right in touch'
('Cepting when I talk too much.)

Maud Boreham

I'LL SHARE YOUR BURDEN

Don't feel so lost, don't retreat into a shell
A time will come when things will turn out well
You may feel now you're not worthy of anybody's love
Have a little faith in the Lord above
You may think people don't care, but believe me, the Lord
                                    will always be there
He'll help you through your suffering, He will share your pain
Maybe when you feel His love for you, you'll feel safe again.

Ann Willbourne

THANK GOD FOR GOD

Walking out one darksome night,
I had a strange sensation.
Imagining our tiny globe complete
with all the nations.
Suspended lonesome in the vastness
of eternal space.
Uniquely peopled with these creatures
called the human race.
My very soul was insecure, pervaded
with unease.
Was our future in the hands of
people just like me?
I know that I'm quite capable of
making bad mistakes.
I trembled much on realising
just what we had at stake.
Many years have passed since then.
Our world is in a shambles.
I no longer feel prepared to
take a risky gamble.
I am glad to know that God is
in complete control.
I don't think man is capable
of taking on that role!

Lyn Coker

TWO HALVES OF THE SAME

Did you think about your birth?
Should you think about your death?
Did you understand all about truth?
Would you recognise any of the lies?

All the religions were created by Man!
Yet all men were created by God!
Most now say 'Who knows what's right?'
So, therefore, they can't know what's wrong!

When will the world finally come to its end?
Death! Your world ending, yet a beginning!
For belief, it maybe will cost you your life!
Don't live for something that will cost your soul!

Kieran Corr

THE FLOTSAM AND JETSAM OF LIFE

I stood on the shore,
As the grey sea rushed in,
The foam - covered waves hit the beach.
The tide brought the cans and the bottles and sticks,
Then carried them far beyond reach.
I thought of the rubbish contained in the sea,
Now covered over, for no-one to see,
The flotsam and jetsam of life.

I stood on a hill,
As the red sun went down,
And shadows fell long on the ground.
I looked at the papers and peelings of fruit,
With crisp packets blowing around.
I thought of the spoiling of countryside green,
Where creatures and wildlife were now only seen,
As the flotsam and jetsam of life.

I stood in the town
Where a girl dressed in black,
Was squatting in front of the square.
A weary brown dog cowered low by her side,
Near her feet, which were swollen and bare.
I thought of the people without any home.
My eyes filled with tears, for they had become,
The flotsam and jetsam of life.

Vicki Robinson

THOUGHTS AT A CONCERT

'Pack up your troubles,' how everybody sang!
The voices rose and filled the room.
I pictured ranks of marching men
Who died before I left the womb.
I saw packed trains, the waved goodbyes,
The troopships and the crowded rail,
I saw the wraiths of Ypres and Somme,
Of Mons and Marne and Passchendaele,
The wretched trenches, deep in mud,
And men in fear of mustard gas.
I saw their khaki stained with blood
And many a stretcher party pass -

    Yet at the concert people sang
    Of what they all had never seen;
    Too young to know of any war
    It might have never ever been -
    Except for this strange echoing.
    And 'Altogether now' - again -
    There flashed the guns of Taganrog,
    The heat and sweat of Alamein.

Oh! Heather with your shyest glance,
And gentle flute's melodious air,
Elspeth with your merry smile
Bright-eyed and dimpled, curling hair -
I prayed that you might never know
The tragic things your elders had,
The sorry mess of Nijmegen,
The bitter cold of Stalingrad.

Stella Shepherd

THE ROUNDABOUT OR WHERE ARE WE GOING

What other carefree feet once stood
on this the central island wilderness,
Eyes gazing across green meadows
now buried beneath tons of tarmac
tonguing out in all directions.
Did someone say: 'Let's rest awhile
before we journey further?'
The roar of progress drowned that one lone voice.

The parks department planted trees
to ease the outward landscape,
but here at the hub
surrounded by dust and noise,
sparse tufts of resurrected grass
thrust through their concrete coffin,
unnoticed by the passing motorists
who take the second turning to the left -
Or is it right?

Barbara Collier

Peace In Our Time

Peace is such a fragile thing
In this turbulent world of ours
So many men of violence
So many many wars
There seems to be no end to it
Nor what their reasons are
These men are never ever pleased
Unless *they're* the ones in power
For power is what it's all about
Dictatorship their aim
That all should be downtrodden
So that these men can reign
There seems such awful ignorance
Of what fairness really means
They think it only matters
That what *they* want comes in reams
Of paper and promises with total disregard
For what is fair to others
In this war torn land of ours
Why can't they be contented
With the world just as it is
They hanker for *possession*
Of a world that isn't theirs
For it belongs to God alone
While we are only tenants
And when he comes again to earth
Those men will pay their penance

Maureen Quirey

FACE TO FACE

When a bus, filled with faces, glides by
I wonder 'Do they worry, do they pray - as I do?'
I think 'Are they all querying why
Transgression persists in this world and failing's not new?'
Stranger regards me with friendly stare,
Peering, a woman, through misty, inanimate glass,
Her eyes say 'I'd know you anywhere!'
But I'm free of suspicion and let that moment pass
Racism conquers this earth, we know,
As though in *pass the parcel*, we circulate the bomb,
Do strangers let inner feelings show?
'When,' I wonder of those eyes 'will Armageddon come?'
Polluting bus waits beside the kerb
Spirit and flesh, it all combines to watch me fumble
For cash - somehow divining orbs disturb
'Oh, do pass on, don't you see I know you not,' I mumble.
Just how can I differentiate
For today the ills of greed land prejudice run rife?
Yet who am I to judge? Do not wait
For me to smile, grown sceptical, wary in this life;
Perfection's my goal yet still I slide,
Sin with all humanity, - those faces on the bus
Gazing out, uncomfortable inside,
That penetrate my skull - announce
'You are still one of us.'

Ruth Daviat

FAITH

How long will we take to find home?
It seems like a thousand light years
I walked barefoot along a jagged edge
To know well the tracks of my tears.

I see great pain of travelling souls
Behind bright painted smiles of a clown,
How long must we suffer loneliness?
Terror of rollercoasters plunging down?

We are ghosts, consigned to wilderness
Tortured by visions, mothers, silver, gold,
We walk in the feet of ancestors still
Our hearts young, our spirits growing old.

Have you suffered so badly, my love?
You must find the strength to hang on,
Brave strangers on peripheries of life
Cling to faith when all hope has gone.

John Farrell

THE MOST BEAUTIFUL WORD

I do not own the stars so how can I give them to you,
The moon is also not mine.
The oceans' flow and ebb could not prove my love is true,
Nor the glory of the sunshine.

Many poets have written words of love through the years,
Far more eloquent than I.
With many words so beautiful to describe just a tear,
Who am I to even try.

My frugal thoughts are shipwrecked, feeble, drowned in the brine,
My heart has totally sunk.
Many have toasted love that is as sweet as red wine,
What chance I? Yours has me drunk.

I have read the books of knowledge that describe 'What is love?'
Dictionaries and thesaurus.
What is special about birds and the wings of a dove,
The most beautiful word is *us!*

Warren Galley

POVERTY

Being poor is difficult,
There's so much to cope with,
But I think that worst of all
Is the bigotry of others.

They focus on the surface,
The old and well-worn clothes,
They think you're not worth more,
It's as though you've chosen this.

They only see the outside,
They miss the good within,
They can't see your potential,
They're so blinkered by their bias.

I'd rather a lack of money,
Than a wealth of prejudice,
And sooner an empty purse,
Than a barrenness of spirit.

Bridget Holding

BREAK BREAD TOGETHER

Let us hold the hands of others
Let us stand in unity
Let us break our bread together
Let us share our meal today.
In our dreams we hold a vision
In our hearts we know the truth
That in breaking bread together
We will find the only way.

There's a light upon our table
That will sparkle in our eyes
As we break our bread together
And we speak in harmony.
In the corner sits a stranger
He is welcomed to our fare
As we break our bread together
We will all be family.

Over every field and nation
Grow the seeds of joy and love
If we all broke bread together
Wars would end and pain would cease.
Let us eat the fruits of concord
Let us drink the kindness cup
Let us break our bread together
One in spirit one in peace.

Eleanor Clarke

ALONG THE WAY...

Among the toils of every day,
Routine that sets the daily way,
A moment's pause is all you need
To think of love,
To heed
To that on which we feed.

It's easy to forget the smile
And sink in custom all the while
In which we cling, as if by this
An open heart
Can live in bliss,
Demeaning the meaning of a kiss.

Amidst the race of daily life,
Where thoughtlessness in each is rife,
A stop to watch the swaying flower
Stills the beat
Of the watch's power
To steal us from our verdant lover.

Soon the road gives way to field
And meadowsweet that this will yield
Is always there but to be seen
In this new beauty,
This new mien.
As this new life is ours to scheme,
To make it real,
Not just a dream.

Andrea Noelle Vaughan

TWO SIDES FOR LIVING

There's a light side and a dark side
now which one will we choose?
Well that's not really difficult
no need to get the blues.

Some are rich and others poor
maybe black or white
It's the heart that really matters
live in peace, or stand and fight?

We don't have to be really saintly
but always do the best we can
Just be helpful and more kindly
be we Mary, Jack or Dan.

The world can be a better place
not all doom and gloom
So just look on the bright side
for *love* there's *always* room.

There are many lonely people
afraid to leave their home
No reason then for living
nor can they ever roam

So let us help each other
and always lend a helping hand
For all the old and needy
make others' life real grand.

For *every* day is really special
so don't let it pass you by
For you *never* can replace it
when it's time for you to die.

Joy Spickermann

I Am

Don't treat me as if I'm stupid
Don't assume I cannot hear
I see you turn your head away
Whenever I am near
You pretend you cannot see me
Every time that you pass by
But I see the truth on your face
I see the look that's in your eyes
You don't know how to treat me
I embarrass you when I'm here
From your heart I feel your pity
From your mind I sense your fear
But if I look within you
Down in your deepest soul
I see that what you feel is guilt
That I, to you, am not a whole
Though on the outside I look different
I'm a person inside, can't you see
I cannot glance then hurry on past
I cannot turn away from me
So spare me some compassion
And just reach out your hand
Touch me with your love and light
Give peace to your fellow man
What man shall sow, so shall he reap
The Lord teaches so you can see
What you give will be returned to you
And the next time you could be me.

Porter Duff

TRUST IN MY SOCIETY

What society? Our babies born addicts and worst
a deadly disease known as AIDS. A good start I say.
Our children of both sexes selling their underdeveloped
bodies to depraved creatures for grub and an added fix
to face the horrors of their world. In their hellish earth
they seek some help from ministering angels on some
occasions makes their plight more lasting and more hellish.
Parents can do this all on their own,
'what more at a stranger's hands.'
Faith in our society, you asked and wished you hadn't
and I just barely started.

Margaret Gleeson Spanos

ANTHONY

Anthony was talented, at the piano and percussion,
but suddenly an illness struck, his brain just ceased to function.
Schizophrenia had taken hold, he had lost the will for life,
the doctors hadn't taken time to get him stabilised.

So he started heavy drinking, he lived from place to place,
as he couldn't keep to all the rules that Councils make for space,
space to shelter in the night, company throughout the day,
in desperation he resolved to take his life away.

Next day he made a visit home, determined to impress.
He shaved his chin, brushed his hair, he dressed to look his best.
He chatted brightly with his folk, but his father felt alarm
but the doctor said 'Those nasty bastards seldom come to harm.'

The next morning the police arrived, they had seen a saddening sight,
a body was found upon the ground, it had fallen from great heights.
The father went to identify that this was his own son,
an inquest into the mentally ill had finally begun.

In Britain we treat them with contempt, the policy is sound,
pretend that they just don't exist, that keeps the costs right down!
The Policy of Community Care so often seems to fail,
the patients need a stable home - lots of loving care.

For Care in Community to help the mental patient
each sufferer must have someone near for company and attention.
This of course drives costs right up, which the country can't afford,
for lower taxes is the cry, the sick can be ignored.

So the country must revert, to pleasant homes with staff,
with resident help in crafts and arts and shows to make us laugh.
For normal health can be restored if society is patient,
to meet the bill to let us cope, and finally become efficient.

Trebor Lien

NEVER MINE

Eight o'clock, I look at my line
This week, please let it be me
A gloved hand presses the button
Down come the numbers - but never mine

Another week without a sign
of a fortune I richly deserve
Why does the money always go
to people whose cares are never mine?

A ticket to misery, so they whine
But what a lot I could achieve
Easier to be happy with millions
Debts all around and never mine

That handsome fellow with looks divine
would notice me, to be sure
if I became rich and famous
His charms wasted, if never mine

Oh joy! Straight away I could resign
My job they say keeps the firm afloat
Although, would they really miss me?
Prospects good, they said, yet never mine!

Just suppose a win so fine
came my way with six lucky numbers
Every material need could be settled
Struggles and joys therefore, never mine

Every day, every week I would recline
After all, what else? It has all been done.
How I'd miss my friends and the old house
and in this dream, happiness is never mine.

Maureen Mills

THE GREY GENERATION

The young man said 'Thank you'
The grey head was bent.
'I was there when they signed for peace' he said.
'Yes . . . thank you for going, for fighting for me.'
'I had no choice - I was sent.'

That young man was rare - he knew
Our bright youth was spent
In France, or the desert - war zones, instead
Of our homes, our careers, our country, our life.
Our nation's choice . . . we were sent.

Fifty years on - don't they care
Our hearts are rent?
With edicts from Europe - cars from Japan
The 'enemy' rules us through business and finance.
Was it for that we were sent?

Old wounds heal, but the scarring
Still omnipresent.
My father dead, our cousin's mind damaged,
Our pensions so small, our experience discarded.
Our lives just for this, we spent?

This is the freedom we sought.
Their freedom to live
Doing things their way, through business, not war
Loving *our* enemies . . . who were sent.
All bought by us, who are spent.

Joyce Goldie

LIFE'S GOAL

What is this game we need to play where no one knows the rule?
A game devised by who knows who,
that's played by sage and fool.
And there again by young and old; by healthy and infirm.
With feats you cannot justify,
nor even gauge their term.

Where chosen men illumine the way and teach where lies the mark.
Yet 'fore their guiding light emerged
the players knew nought but dark.
So how might they perceive their goal, or, we discern our try.
Where rests the target of our test?
Who deems we satisfy?

For each of us who strive to win does someone taste defeat?
Or, granted be a second try,
perchance just lost a heat?
And are the odds the same for all? The pitfalls equal sown?
There are so many ponderables,
can fact be ever known?

But, is the truth so shrouded that the players cannot see?
Or, the message there so ancient
that it's cloaked in mystery?
No! Though players may be varied; numerous as the stars above,
there's a moment even to them all,
a chance to share their love.

Malcolm F Rowlatt

Man Destroys Man

Man destroys man or so they say,
It's become so true this very day,
A drunk will die from the invention of alcohol.

A child will die from the invention of the car,
A person will die from the invention of the boat.
We could all die from the invention of the bomb.

How true it is, I could go on and on -
Like dinosaurs before us, we could fade away.

But population should stop that,
Most of us live long, but in between that,
Man destroys man,
It goes on and on.

Christine Miller

JUST LOOK AROUND

If we who would destroy the world
Would stop to look around.
Why pick a rose and crush its petals,
Then throw them to the ground.

Jacqueline Sanderson

The World

Has society gone mad?
The old man asked
With a tear in his wrinkled eye
It's changed so much since I was a lad
I really don't know why.
You could have walked the streets
Without any fear
And spoke to all around
But now when you walk
You suspect everyone
And listen to every sound
Children could play on the streets
Without being watched
And women just the same
But with the sick minded perverts
That are running about
Anyone is now fair game.
With mind bending drugs that banish reasonable thought
And make it seem alright to be bad
And when they are caught the court lets them off
The whole thing becomes so sad.
While pensioners starve
And die of the cold
And are abused by muggers and the rest
Prisoners behind bars can live life to the full
And have food and education of the best
With the world gone mad and in such a state
And for life I've lost my zest
I just can't wait for the day to come
When I have my final rest.

James McErlean

HEAR MY PRAYER

There is a church, up on a hill
Where peace and love you can instil.
As through the door, you enter there
To kneel and say a loving prayer.
To ask that all wars, will cease
That once more, we could live in peace.
Oh Lord, why is man so full of greed,
Always taking more than his need?
Why can't he learn, how to share?
Just maybe then, he'll begin to care
About humanity and his fellow man
To live in harmony as best he can.
I say this prayer for all today,
That you send your light, so they'll find their way.

Audrey Walker

INSIGHT

Everywhere inadequate fools believe their lies, with scant
intelligence to disguise from me, their lack of individuality.
Contemptuous of restricted thoughts that never aspire beyond
idle reports. All seemingly worship an abandoned sky, the parched
arid land of Appolo's eyes, whereas I; when watching the drift
of nature's shroud embrace every pregnant ponderous cloud.
I draw pleasure when the witless complain, and scurry like rats
from the lashing rain.

Yet this ruling darker side doth conflict, my compassion whose
end could not be found; except to that of mankind where I restrict,
without strife, the reciprocated emotions that others feel bound.
To them, when the feeling is upon me, no blasphemous words
will suffice.
A changing solace mutates my will and as a god would sacrifice
the perpetrators who render down all that is good; sweep clear
the dust of their wasted souls, scrub so all abroad is clean,
then stand forever joyous at the scene. Call forth the like to populate:
finally, serenity, the victor of my dark, will let me walk at last in green.

D F Baker

A Changed Society

I remember well the day
when keys were left in doors:
Cars could sit unlocked
and the elderly were safe.

Families enjoyed quality time:
Neighbours called to chat;
People helped each other out
and simple things gave pleasure.

Now we live in a frantic age,
with fast foods and quick carry-outs;
Pressurised to buy and pay by card
whether we need the item or not.

Crime is rife, no-one is safe,
Pollution is serious, no job is secure;
Churches are empty, the Lord's day is abused,
Biblical standards are slipping fast.

The decline in morals is sad to see:
Family breakdown is almost the norm;
How sorry I feel for the next generation,
Who have missed out on much that was simple and good.

Technology has reached an amazing stage,
There *seems* no limit to what man can do;
Self-sufficiency brags, 'We don't need *you* God.'
And down the slippery slope we go.

Deceivers there are in the name of Christ,
Claiming so much and fooling many;
This is the way Christ said it would be.
It's a sign of the times, so watch carefully! *(Matt:24)*

One day the Lord will return for His own,
'Twill be too late then to call on His name;
Every race, colour and creed
will stand before the judgement throne.

Shirley Hay

SWEET VINE OF LIFE

You are the sea from which all waters flow
Sweet breath of life, you quicken, you enthral
You are the flame that sets all hearts aglow
The son who lights the fire within the soul
You are the source of all we need to know
The voice who guides us, calls us to be saved
You are the sower, we the seeds you sow
Yours is the life which frees us from the grave
Yours is the touch which cleanses us with light

Sweet vine of life
Sweet vine of life.

Cassandra Hazeley-Wilson

Tomorrow's World

Today a man-made hard society -
layered by destructive greed -
at war with want and need -
unseen the outcome.

Spendthrift we have been
with all God's bounty.
Industry's true cost uncounted
questions the quality of life created -
before tomorrow dawns - debate it well.
Beliefs and mores now deemed old-fashioned.
Laws broken with impunity.
Uncontrolled our passions.
Self rules our ways.
Speed our compass range exceeds,
a true direction is man's need.

God is man's Constant.
He gave us light and life.
No creed or church imprisons Him -
our God is everywhere.
In love He calls - 'My children come to Me,
I hold the key to life's fulfilment.'

His gifts of faith, of trust and love
are for man's daily use.
If actioned into simple deeds they multiply
to greatness.
Our sharing of earth's fruitfulness
may harvest for all people a new tomorrow.
Brothers of one blood by God created,
Of His earth, inheritors.
Prayer is mighty - God hear our prayer
for our tomorrow's world.

Christina Crowe

A Song For Lonely Hearts

When lonely hearts can rest,
Upon the sleepy mountain peaks
The silvery wind will sing
Melodies of peace and calm.

Alive, with tranquil minds
We search within our souls
For something, beyond life's facade,
Whilst along the quiet path we stride.

In dells, the delicate ferns will hide
Their shimmering leaves from storms
And breathe the cool, refreshing air,
Shaded beneath the oaks and pines

From myriads of raindrops
Cast from ashen skies.
Come sing again, oh voice of God,
Sing again.

Gail Farrell

My Christian Faith

My Christian faith
Has seen me through.
To live, and love,
My life with you.

What time is left
Is simply free.
My heart to give,
My love for Thee.

A life has passed,
I know not whence.
What's left for me,
Is 'Heaven-sent'.

The future's bright,
Or so it seems
With so much hope,
And not just dreams.

So take 'good heart',
And trust in me,
Let's share what's left
. . . *in harmony* . . .

Michael John Swain

The Preacher

In long black overcoat and trilby hat,
He stands Bible in hand,
Shouting out the word of God,
Stored from within the recess of his mind,
Quoting out the scriptures,
Chapter and verse,

People pass by without one look,
Ignoring his cries of woe and damnation,
That will surely fall on those,
Who choose to ignore the word of God,
Adults go about their daily chores,
Deaf to the vocal chords that echo around them,

See the guilty faces, heads hung low,
In denial of the words,
Rather than a confrontation face to face,
There in all weathers torrential rain,
And the cold hand of winter,
Nothing deters him,

He is not afraid to speak out,
To be a lone disciple,
Preaching from the middle of the High Street,
In this large town,
Secretly from afar I admire him,
For the enthusiasm his living Lord provokes within him,

For his faith to stand up and be counted,
Our Lord more important to him,
Than the image of rejection he reaps in,
Known by some as the mad preacher,
He deflects these stones,
By promoting only love and peace.

Not one person not even I,
Acknowledge having heard his word,
I would like him to know I believe,
In my mind I ask that others hear his words,
And what he has to say,
This preacher of our modern times.

Ann G Wallace

REFLECTIONS

Society changes with the times so they say,
But surely life was better yesterday,
Everything moving at a much slower pace,
Not stressed out, trying to win in today's rat race.

Fewer cars on the roads, not bumper to bumper,
Time to sit and knit a cheery red jumper,
Good entertainment, a night at the flicks,
No sex or violence, 'cos the censor said 'Nix.'

Today on the screen we see life in the raw,
Do your own thing, no rules like before,
With all this freedom does anything last?
We felt more secure in those days in the past.

Back then family life, it was king,
Third finger, left hand, wearing a ring,
Babies born to a husband and wife,
Relationship to last the rest of your life.

But today in the atmosphere of moral decline,
Anything goes, who cares if you step out of line,
Have children with one partner and then with another,
Marriage, a bit of paper, why bother?

A mad dash for the few jobs that may be on offer,
Otherwise it's down to the *social* to put a few pounds in the coffer,
Beware of the food on your plate, 'cos though it may fill you,
The way things are today, it may well just kill you.

So then you ask, from here, where can we go?
I believe to the Lord, in fact I just know,
If we follow His ways, look to the one who's above,
He'll sort it all out and show us His love.

Pauline Wilkins

I Wonder

Sitting on a cliff top, as have many more
Not in this time, not in yours
But as hundreds did before
My hair is gently blowing
As the wind blows from the sea
Sitting here on the cliff top
With my arms clasped round my knees

Listening to the lapping, lapping of the seas
The rolling of the pebbles
As the tide comes in and out
Daring other noises
To break through stillness round about

Did our forefathers sit and wonder
If they could reach above the sky
Or explore the deepest ocean
Just as many people try

Could they have walked along the seashore
And thrown pebbles in the sea
Just like little children
Yes as you and me
For it's true to tell they never knew
Such wonders down there lie
Or man, could ever reach, beyond the bluest sky

Beneath the sea and pebbles
Now many trinkets lie
Lost through time eternal
Like hidden wonders in the sky
Dearest father of all children
Pray keep your secrets big or small
Until man can unearth them
For the love of one and all

Susan Goldsmith

UNROBED IN ULSTER

Clothing this province's contours
Like warm mantles
Unfurled and deliberately draped
Across naked topography,
Our town-scapes settle.
And in November's dusk,
Interspersed and silhouetted steeples
Stand prominent and proud,
Marking the common thread
Which fastens
Place to place
And creed to creed.

But in these, too,
Is bred that spurious incisiveness
Which helps man distinguish
Cloth from cloth
And faith from faith,
Championing supremacy for one
Over another.
And I am reminded of
Man's first disobedience
At that time
When once we all stood
Unrobed
In paradise.

Peter Taylor

Contemporary Commination

We have killed custom,
Kind mother of harmony;
Nourished on novelty,
Nervous nursemaid,
Hourly paid,
We sicken secretly.

We have unseated stability,
Sweet sister of serenity;
Side-saddle she rode;
Although she had grace,
Too slow was her pace:
We've toppled tranquillity.

We have slain service,
Strong second of loyalty;
Our foe is fidelity:
Each pledges his hand
To his own stand:
We die in disunity.

We have drugged conscience,
Door-keeper of destiny;
His post was solitary:
We stormed his keep,
And now he's asleep,
We consider collectively.

We have dethroned love,
Queen of capacities;
She brooks no rivalry:
Without her reign
All is in vain:
We perish perfectly.

Trudi Yates Morgan

CHANGING FOR THE BETTER

Money makes the world go round
People worry if the pound goes up or down
'Business is business,' we hear them say
Consuming every minute of their day
People striving to reach perfection
Pay no-one else any attention
Pursuing selfish motives in all they do
No consideration for what they put others through
'Tis the people who love those they hurt the most
Pushing away the ones who would be close.

If they took time to consider others for a change
They'd have nothing to lose and so much to gain
If only they could know they do the wrong thing
If an alarm in their conscience would only ring
Letting them know that what they do is not right
Then surely a new beginning would be in sight
To give to others is the greatest gift of all
It can elevate you to ten feet tall
Like taking time to spend with your mother
Is a wonderful tribute of concern for another
To aid someone less fortunate than yourself
You'll find you receive when you give to someone else.

Too many people have set the pace
If the world caught up it would be a better place
A future for our children would be crystal clear
If they follow our example they'd have nothing to fear
If I could change the world, for this I'd pray
That things would get better every day
If people would stop taking and begin to give
This world would be a better place to live.

Twinny

GOD'S PLAN WAS PERFECT

God made the world, a beautiful place
Fit for everyone in the human race,
But man allowed the devil full sway
Which was for man a very bad day.

For this set the seal for all mankind,
Man turned their backs on God, who was kind,
They listened to the devil's voice,
Which helped the devil to rejoice.

This was just what the devil wanted,
And no matter how much they ranted,
The devil went on and tightened his grip
And laughter and scorn he let rip.

And ever since Adam and Eve that day
Let the old devil have his own way,
People have wavered and followed suit,
The devil has got another recruit.

However, there is a way back to God,
We don't need to walk where others trod,
Our God is loving and kind to all
Who trust Him and answer His call.

He wants His world to be a better place
For all of us in the human race,
It is up to us to play our part,
The best thing to do is give Him our heart.

Then live for God each and every day,
We all have a wonderful part to play,
So let's make our world a better place
For everyone throughout the human race.

Vera G Taylor

Our Modern Age

Leaders heedless of the call
to be followers of peace,
care they not who fight and fall
as hostilities increase,

Where the maimed and dying cling
to the living, who must mourn
while the new Dark Ages ring
with the cries of the forlorn.

Free abortions by request:
take away a human life
that will never know the zest
or experience the strife.

Cloning sheep and cattle, now
duplicating humans in
their lost state, not caring how
dwells the living soul within.

Earthquake, famine, flood and fire,
these engulf our human race,
caught by camera entire,
instantly before our face.

Far beyond earth's atmosphere
unmanned craft are ever bound
for some distant, unseen sphere,
silent to our human sound.

Dorothy Headland

WATERMARK

A deep truth as only we know, others will guess,
a brand on our soul
simple clear and for ever
an acid test no less.
A hidden signal to light revealed
visionary ghosts peering,
quiet to its meaning and checks
might even be God-fearing.
Beneath an evil can good emerge
to peel back the stigma only ignorance knows,
that stamp which reforms
our redeemer's good teachings thro' light shall expose.

Tom Griffiths

A Dream For Us All

A breeze uplifting,
the dusk looms near
thoughts in our minds
of friends who were dear
friends no longer with us
who sadly passed away
we are deemed to meet
another place another day.
A deep breath is taken
No sigh of relief
a gentle stroll back
to the land of belief
where people wish for happiness
not illness, no more pain
where we yearn to live in harmony
we don't want war, but peace again
if only it came true
and our children were okay
to walk the streets at night
and play safely in the day
a world we all dream of
but a far distant cry
some day it could happen:
We can all but try.

Jane Smith

What Is Important

Opinion, self-inflated and unquestionable
Feeds the treadmill which turns relentlessly
Providing motivation for material gain.
And then what?
Do we turn in on ourselves?
Grasping greedily at the ever increasing standards in our lives?
Or: do we radiate outwards?
Spreading a little of ourselves into the darkness and despair of
                                                                         other lives
Lives which fleetingly intrude through broadcast images
They invade our compassion.
We pretend we care.
Momentarily we offer sympathy
Before withdrawing into our silk cocoons
Undisturbed in its comfortable warmth;
As usual doing nothing,
Giving nothing,
And -
Counting for nought.

Wendy Brennan

WORLD VISION

Time is folding up like the golden pages
of a good, old, story book
All is fading, failing, falling, rolling into a ball of fire

>Man has done his job
>Played his part in destroying the world

Cast your eyes on the sulphuric and copper coloured leaves
the yellowing sand, the mustard sun, the autumn moon,
they all signify and symbolise, the end in our twilight years

>The hand of man extinguishes and obliterates
>all preparation for future generations

Feel and smell the heat of scorching sun
Dry, brittle, withering
See and taste the difference in the once fertile land
Hear the thirsty land belching;
all are atmospheric signs showing this world in decline

>But man does not hear, his eyes cannot see
>because, he is not listening with his heart

Fewer become the visits of the songbirds at our windows
The elements rage
Water, wind and fire, as set in array, by man, they battle for supremacy
trying to decide on snow, tornado or hell fire

>O man of clay. What can be said?
>Why? For by melting down the earth's inner layer
>man has this task done

We cease to think of each other. Our goal in life, here and now
says look out for number one, no one else matters
not the children of tomorrow

> The signals we ignore, of our world systematically
> spinning into global deterioration and decay
> Is this the scenario we are leaving for our children?

Rosetta Stone

MARRIAGE

Marriage is just another word,
In a dictionary today,
'Cos a lot of young couples aren't interested,
In making promises to obey.

It used to mean, after courting,
That sweethearts made a vow,
To love one another, 'til death do part,
But it seldom happens now.

Big weddings cost a fortune,
That lovers can't afford,
So the decision to live together,
Is made of their own accord.

So now, they've no anniversaries to celebrate,
Or any alimony to pay out,
But still, for the sake of their children,
Marriage is best, without a doubt.

Jean Hendrie

GOD ONLY KNOWS

Does God ever wish he'd never made people?
Or gold,
Or bishops,
Or lofty church steeple?

Does he groan at the endless sinful lists,
At man's futility
When words
Turn to fists?

Does he ever get mad
When they slag down His son.
While using His birthday
For boozing and fun?

Does he ponder all this,
And what it shows?
The answer, my friend,
Is God only knows . . .

Anthony Stern

WILL THE WORLD?

Will the world get any better?
Or will we keep on this way?
Will difference lie in tomorrow?
Or will it be the same as today?

Will the generation who are born,
By those who decided to pray,
Keep going as their parents,
Or just go out and play?

Will the world live in peace?
Or this way just stay?
Will it all just end in war?
Will the world collapse like unhardened clay?

I hope that in a few years time,
These questions will go day by day -
I hope they'll be answered,
And in a very good way.

Samantha Douglas (12)

CIRCLE OF LIGHT

When creating the circles,
We guide the journey of our children,
Not knowing the moments of life ahead;
Providing support to maintain the circle,
Hoping as the path of the circle grows;
That they will link with other circles;
So creating circles linked by generations,
Linked circles are far stronger for
Life's moments than squares.

B J Tallowin

FORGIVENESS

I picked up the newspaper,
Was just browsing through,
I really wanted the crossword to do,
When out of the pages a story I read,
'Old lady beaten up and left for dead.'

I read to the end,
It was so unbelievable,
To do her such harm,
Was just inconceivable.
She was going to visit a friend who was sick.
They knocked her to the ground,
And ran away quick.

Forty pounds in her purse was all she had,
A small price to pay for all that bad.
But in her hospital bed all beaten and bruised,
She prayed to God, she was not confused.

'Please forgive the people who caused me this pain,
They need your help before they do this again.'
Her thoughts full of pity and not a cross word,
Made me think of something I had once heard.
And then I remembered this gracious line,
'To err is human but to forgive is divine.'

Jennifer Brewer

Twelve Days Of Xmas

Twelve corrupt jurors,
Eleven plus,
Ten o'clock news,
Nine to five,
Ate heartily while others starved,
Seven deadly sins,
Six counties,
Five year plan,
Four horsemen of the apocalypse,
Three ring circus,
Too late to change,
One forgotten child.

David Atkinson

REALITY

For the monks in their hooded garb,
The monastery is a tranquil place.
It's a perfect secret idyll,
To avoid the humdrum rat race.

For those who live and pray there.
It's a sublime way of life.
A haven hidden from the world,
Free from care and daily strife.

It's a serene and peaceful refuge,
But hiding from reality can't be right.
Even monks devout and saintly,
Must realise this world's sad plight.

Pam Lewis

THINK OF TOMORROW

The warm rays of sunshine brighten the day
But what will it be like in the future I say?
Will the breeze gently blow from the sea to the shore?
Or will it be unfit to live here any more?
To swim in the river, the coolness I feel,
Dare I not touch it in case I am ill?
Will the grass be as green and the sky be as blue?
When you cut down the trees, do you know what you do?
Don't turn the land to desert, we can't live off the sand
We want to grow things to eat, on green and pleasant land.
Get rid of all the chemicals that make the earth so bad.
To look around at greyness is very, very sad.
God gave us land to live and dwell
So don't make it a living hell.

Evelyn Ingram

A Fear Of The Future

To what do we owe our earth -
Devastation of all growth?
Destruction of new beginnings?
An emptiness of all so old?
Forgotten in the mind of time?
:- Not that to come or pass.
Should we not cherish,
Love and protect our mother?
We are children of the future
And of dying nature.
Employ the orb,
For it needs protection,
From us so dominant,
Change the inevitable
As we will proceed the tidings of goodwill.
Not so a fear for us but for galaxy's globe,
Hidden behind darkened space.
Help us reunite the health
In all that will live in she.

Deborah Hughes

Friend

A light in the darkness
an answer to prayer
a friend of sinners
Jesus has compassion and care

The leper and the lonely
the crippled and the blind
Jesus mixed with whoever
to bring hope to mankind

An example of friendship
in a society of sin
an example of true love
with no tut-tut-tutting

Jesus wants the believer
to come alongside
those who are lost
and hurting inside

To have faith in society
and our fellow man
the Christian's plight
is to befriend all he can

God loves the world
and demonstrated to all
that he brought hope to society
that was marred by the fall

God is the answer
in the society we live
the believer is the vessel
to the world they must give.

Trevor Brammah

PEACE - PERFECT PEACE

Peace at home among the children;
Peace among the adults too;
Peace among our friends and colleagues;
Peace to make our dreams come true.

Peace for every race and nation;
Peace for Muslims, Christians, Jews;
Peace for every creed and colour;
Peace, the universal news.

Peace to every state and country;
Peace with justice let us bring;
Peace in the heart of every leader;
Peace, in harmony let us sing.

Monica O'Sullivan

INNOCENT EYES

Pitiful faces, clearly say
Who cares? Who cares?
Tears drop so slowly
From innocent eyes
Wide with deep fears!
It's pointless screaming,
Nobody hears.

Trapped in cruel chains,
Helpless 'sex slaves'
From a very young age!
Once loved and cherished,
Now abused and ravished
By men's evil desires,
Suffering gross pain!

Molested and alone
In this desolate place,
Rejected and debased,
Hungry for real love.
Deep memories of home.
'Where are my friends
When I need them most?'

Almighty God Our Father,
Fill us with compassion
To reach the outstretching hands
Of precious children in despair.
Show us the way
To make a stand!
Not tomorrow, but today!

Marjorie Boyes

Don't Ever Look Back

Don't ever look back, I remember
That's what my mother said
Don't ever look back she told me
Keep looking forward instead
Travel through life's highway
Don't take the lonely road
Always accept the hand of a friend
To help you lighten the load
Look forward to the future
Don't dwell on the past
You've only got one lifetime
And the years go by so fast
Don't look back on the memories
That only make you sad
Look forward to the happy times
And that will make you glad
I know my years are ending, she said
And for me you'll soon wear black
But I want you to look forward
And don't you ever look back
So I'll keep going onward
And give it all I've got
Making sure I take perfect aim
I'll give it my best shot
One day we'll be in paradise
On God's heavenly track
I hope I can smile at her and say
Thanks to you Mum I never looked back

J Robinson

HOUSE BUILDERS

Let's bless this house for it will rise
where an older house once stood,
and on a plot that dates back even further.

Though the actual earth has turned so many times
and the air blows fresh on every breeze,
some echoes still remain to tell of living history.

For apathy and love, and birth and death,
and all our human spectra in between
have graced this place with character

and there are shadows of ghosts that once were folk
who walked this space of universe, yet each one
using their different walls and different doors.

So when again these worlds collide, cold,
upon a midnight stair, we'll nod their presence, but,
brick by brick, project our own designs upon tomorrow.

Stephen Eric Smyth

Our Society

Years ago your next door neighbour
Was also your best friend
They would help you out whenever
Let you borrow things or lend
Today's neighbours are always feuding
Over boundary lines or the like
Complaining when you play your music
Or where your child rides his bike
Many people are no longer courteous
Good manners don't exist like before
We used to all pass the time of day
And always hold open the door
Nothing was too much trouble
The customer was treated right
Today many sales assistants are not bothered
And can be very rude and impolite
Our homes are now like fortresses
Fitted with multi locks and an alarm
Crime is at an all time high
We must protect ourselves from harm
What is happening to our society?
Don't we care about others anymore?
Can't we live together happily?
Do we have to be at war?
Are we all becoming selfish?
More thought for others is not too much to give
Stop all the pain and petty bickering
Let us make the world a better place to live

Linda A Brown

INFORMATION

We hope you have enjoyed reading this book - and that you will continue to enjoy it in the coming years.

If you like reading and writing poetry drop us a line, or give us a call, and we'll send you a free information pack.

Write to :-
**Triumph House Information
1-2 Wainman Road
Woodston
Peterborough
PE2 7BU
(01733) 230749**